NASHV
Food Crawls

Holly Stewart

TOURING *the* **NEIGHBORHOODS**
ONE BITE *&* **LIBATION** *at a* **TIME**

Globe
Pequot

ESSEX, CONNECTICUT

Globe
Pequot

An imprint of Globe Pequot, the trade division of
The Rowman & Littlefield Publishing Group, Inc.
4501 Forbes Blvd., Ste. 200
Lanham, MD 20706
www.rowman.com

Distributed by NATIONAL BOOK NETWORK

British Library Cataloguing in Publication Information available

Library of Congress Cataloging-in-Publication Data

Names: Stewart, Holly (Holly N.), author.
Title: Nashville food crawls : touring the neighborhoods one bite &
  libation at a time / Holly Stewart.
Description: Essex, Connecticut : Globe Pequot, [2024] | Series: Food
  crawls | Includes index.
Identifiers: LCCN 2023048086 (print) | LCCN 2023048087 (ebook) |
  ISBN 9781493045143 (paperback) | ISBN 9781493045150 (epub)
Subjects: LCSH: Restaurants—Tennessee—Nashville—Guidebooks. | Bars
  (Drinking establishments)—Tennessee—Nashville—Guidebooks. |
  Nashville (Tenn.)—Description and travel. | Nashville (Tenn.)—
  Guidebooks. | LCGFT: Guidebooks.
Classification: LCC TX907.3.T2 S74 2024 (print) | LCC TX907.3.T2
  (ebook) | DDC 647.95768/55—dc23/eng/20231221
LC record available at https://lccn.loc.gov/2023048086
LC ebook record available at https://lccn.loc.gov/2023048087

⬭™ The paper used in this publication meets the minimum requirements
of American National Standard for Information Sciences—Permanence of
Paper for Printed Library Materials, ANSI/NISO Z39.48-1992.

Contents

Introduction

IT'S NASHVILLE, Y'ALL! Home of the hot chicken, barbecue, buttery biscuits . . . and that's just breakfast! Nashville has always been a creative hub, and has continued to attract artists of all kinds to our ever-growing city (myself included). Throughout this book, I will introduce you to my favorite Nashville classics alongside a few newbies that continue to shape our restaurant scene. I hope to show you that there is so much more to this city than country music and fried chicken, though I do love both of those things.

My goal in creating this guide was to highlight the special places where I continue to dine and recommend to friends and family time and time again. Nashville just keeps growing. Areas that were once nothing but a parking lot not all that long ago are now home to high rises and high-end restaurants. Our new soccer team has created a different kind of community within our city and the music scene brings in artists from all kinds of genres. Our art scene is steadily growing, with warehouses designed for makers, and small art galleries becoming more commonly integrated into new developments. And just outside the bustling city are miles of trails, waterfalls, and hikes to explore. Companies continue to move their headquarters to Nashville, which creates a love-hate relationship for many, but in turn has skyrocketed our growth and made the city a desirable place to open a new restaurant.

Whether you're a local or a tourist, I hope you discover your new favorite restaurant, dive, or cafe. Nashville is quite a spread-out city, so expect to take a few ride-shares to get from neighborhood to neighborhood! I start this book off on the east side of town, where I spend the majority of my time. So go ahead and start marking your favorites!

Follow the Icons

 CHICKEN: Whether it's hot, fried, or smoked, the chicken at this place is a dish you don't want to miss. What can we say, we're famous for it. Everyone does it a bit differently, and it's delicious.

 BURGER: There's a lot of amazing burgers in this town. It's honestly impossible to pick a favorite, but if I *had* to choose, this place would be on my list. Do me a favor, though—go try them all and report back!

 CHEERS!: We're a drinking town with a music problem, as they say. Be sure to check this place out if you're lookin' to get a little buzzed in more of a bar setting. Typically, you can find that in a lot of places, but this is one of my top choices.

 MUSIC: This establishment has live music! The perfect complement to any good meal. I recommend checking the schedule prior to arrival.

 GNO: As in, girls' night out. I ten out of ten recommend this place for all your bachelorette parties, reunions, sixtieths, etc.

 LIL' FANCY: Pinkies up! This place is a little more upscale than your average honky tonk. Perfect for dressing up and feeling special before you head out for the night!

 PUP FRIENDLY: Bring your furry friends! These places are all dog-friendly patios. Woof! Be sure to check on patio availability at the more formal sit-down restaurants.

 TOP PICK: You've come across a star! This restaurant is one of my top picks!

THE FIVE POINTS CRAWL

1. **I DREAM OF WEENIE**, 113 S. 11TH ST., NASHVILLE, (615) 226-2622, HTTPS://WWW.FACEBOOK.COM/IDREAMOFWEENIE

2. **ROSEMARY & BEAUTY QUEEN**, 1102 FORREST AVE., NASHVILLE, (615) 730-7700, HTTPS://WWW.ROSEMARYANDBEAUTYQUEEN.COM

3. **FIVE POINTS PIZZA**, 1012 WOODLAND ST., NASHVILLE, (615) 915-4174, HTTPS://FIVEPOINTSPIZZA.COM/EAST-NASHVILLE

4. **MARGOT CAFE & BAR**, 1017 WOODLAND ST., NASHVILLE, (615) 227-4668, HTTPS://WWW.MARGOTCAFE.COM

5. **URBAN COWBOY**, 1603 WOODLAND ST., NASHVILLE, (347) 840-0525, HTTPS://WWW.URBANCOWBOY.COM

6. **DINO'S**, 411 GALLATIN AVE., NASHVILLE, (615) 226-3566, HTTPS://WWW.DINOSNASHVILLE.COM

7. **BUTCHER & BEE**, 902 MAIN ST., NASHVILLE, (615) 226-3322, HTTPS://BUTCHERANDBEE.COM

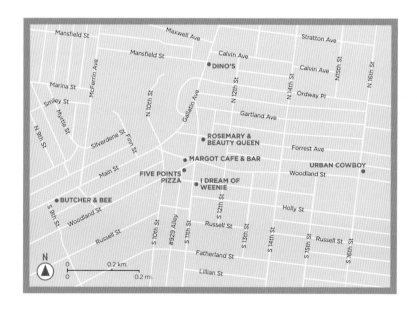

Five Points

Quirk and Community

The heart of East Nashville has a "come as you are" feel; it is home to the Tomato Arts Festival, dive bars, casual joints, and one of my favorite restaurants. Five Points keeps things down-to-earth. As Nashville grows, this neighborhood and its people hold on to the small businesses that brought this side of town to life. Here, if you look, you'll find the best live shows and musicians at no-frill venues, inclusive people, a historic home you dream of buying that you wish you bought ten years ago, and cheap beer. I find this neighborhood perfect for exploring during the early hours of the night and staying out until as late as Five Points decides. Book yourself a dinner, or find somewhere more casual, bar hop here and there, and end the evening with a slice of pizza or a cheese-burger, and karaoke.

1

I DREAM OF WEENIE

I DREAM OF WEENIE is an East Nashville right of passage. This stationary hot dog stand operates out of a vintage yellow VW love bus. It's all parts quirky and delicious. Grab yourself a charcoal grilled weenie, a Cheerwine (a southern cherry cola), and a bag of chips. There are just a few colorfully painted picnic tables scattered around in the grass—since people mostly take their hot dogs to go, I've never had an issue finding a place to sit. Though if it does happen to be crowded, you can grab a provided picnic blanket in the box set out by the VW.

My go to order here is the classic Frank and to the Point, topped with diced onions, relish, ketchup, and mustard. Runner-up would go to the Rebel Yelp, a weenie topped with mustard, Tennessee hot chow-chow (a sweet and spicy relish made with onions, cabbage, and peppers), jalapenos, and chopped red onions.

I Dream of Weenie loves to get creative with their daily specials based on seasonal fruits and veggies. Definitely do not miss the Vidalia goat cheese or truffle mac and cheese weenie! If you're lucky enough to stop by on a Sunday, you can treat yourself to their famous Weenie Brunch, featuring a list of six different breakfast weenies. I go for the French Toast Weenie, a french toasted hot dog bun with breakfast sausage links, maple syrup, and powdered sugar. The Triple H, a hashbrown casserole weenie, is not one to skip either. Grab yourself a Genie Weenie tee on your way out, and take a photo in front of this lovable hot dog establishment.

2 ROSEMARY & BEAUTY QUEEN

If anyone were to ask me what my go-to bar in East Nashville is, I would immediately say **ROSEMARY & BEAUTY QUEEN**. Located in a converted historic home, this place was built with the goal of making patrons feel as if they're at a house party, just with better drinks. Take in the dark wood and green velvet vibes as you enter the living room. Order a cocktail (they always come in a unique glass!) and make your way out back into a scene you wish was your backyard. Find your way into the back building to boogie all night, or head up to the rooftop deck and people watch over all of Five Points—you're bound to see some interesting encounters.

Out of the Rosemary kitchen you'll find oysters on the half shell and a slew of tacos, crunchwraps, and other Mexican bites. Rosemary is great for anyone looking for a casual bite and hang earlier in the evening, meeting with friends, or dancing under the disco ball. You will always find good energy and a friendly crowd while hanging out at this lively gathering spot in the heart of Five Points.

3 FIVE POINTS PIZZA

FIVE POINTS PIZZA feels like the heart of East Nashville to me. When the owners began this adventure, there was nowhere in the neighborhood to grab a slice and a beer. This casual eatery is known for its New York–style pizza. They use New York–style dough made daily from scratch, aged in-house, and always hand tossed. I often find myself there for the $12 weekday lunch special, where I'll get a slice of prosciutto and basil; a classic Italian side salad with romaine lettuce, red onion, mushrooms, black olives, grape tomatoes, and a creamy balsamic; plus a soda of my choice. Other times I'll be at the late-night pizza window, which is open until 1:00 a.m. Sunday through Thursday and until 3:00 a.m. Friday and Saturday.

Whatever you do while dining here, do not leave without ordering the garlic knots! The amount of garlic they use is an absolute blessing. Though it's nearly impossible to choose my favorite whole pie, my top three would have to be the classic Old World (fresh mozzarella, tomato sauce, and fresh basil), the Rocket Pie (arugula tossed in lemon vinaigrette, oven-roasted tomatoes, whole roasted garlic cloves, cracked black pepper, and both fresh and shredded mozzarella), and the Vodka Sauce Pie (house-made vodka tomato cream sauce, prosciutto di Parma, spinach, mushrooms, red

onions, fresh basil, minced garlic, and fresh mozzarella). If you aren't in the East Nashville area, Five Points Pizza has a second location in West Nashville on Charlotte Pike.

4

MARGOT CAFE & BAR

Say bonjour to **MARGOT CAFE & BAR**! My eyes light up when I start talking about this special place. Back in 2001, owner and chef Margot McCormack was the pioneer of East Nashville restaurants. Margot turned this once 1930s service station into the coziest, most welcoming, French, farm-to-table restaurant

that the town can't get enough of. The charming setting is decorated with copper pans, well-loved furniture, and vintage plates. There's also a phenomenal staff that knows every detail of the daily changing menu. Whether you're looking to celebrate with a special someone, pop in for a glass of wine and fresh focaccia, or have an intimate dinner with a group of friends, this is your spot!

As mentioned earlier, the Margot menu changes every single day! But don't worry, it's always fantastic. Throughout you'll notice homage to local farmers, seasonal dishes, ingredients that appear throughout the menu, and reimagined classic French dishes. I'll steer you toward any salad with butter lettuce, warm olives, any and all soups, and anything having to do with a pork chop. Oh, and dessert. Do not leave without a house-made ice cream, fruit tart, or mousse—and throw in an aperitif. An evening at Margot can instantly make an ordinary day feel like a little holiday away from home, even just for a night.

5

URBAN COWBOY

The historic Queen Anne Victorian mansion, once a family home, is now one of the hippest and well-designed bed and breakfasts. If you're looking for a low-key spot with great cocktails, natural wine, pizza, and an effortlessly cool Nashville scene, you must check it out! You've likely seen photos on Instagram of the vintage southwestern decor and mesmerizing woodwork. Out back you will find Public House, former horse stable and backyard, now turned bar and restaurant. URBAN COWBOY strives to ensure that their patrons who come in as strangers leave as friends, and you will be sure to pick up on this energy as soon as you enter.

Public House has an incredible long-term resident—Roberta's Pizza from Brooklyn, New York. For those who love a fresh, air bubbled, slightly charred, personal pizza, this is one of the best. There's something so comfortable about sitting in the backyard, splitting pizzas with friends, cozying up in a flannel blanket if needed, and enjoying conversation by the many fire pits. All the vibes without the fuss. Seating is first come, first served, so I recommend showing up a little earlier than you originally planned to scout out a spot!

For drinks, take a look at their curated cocktail list, or head inside the hotel and grab a bottle of natural wine. The aesthetics of it all might have you leaning toward their P.H. Old Fashioned with house-made bitters, or if in the chilly months, their hot toddy always hits the spot.

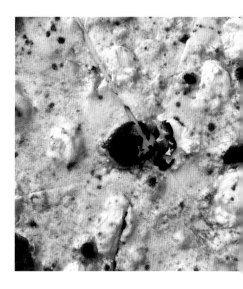

TIP

IF THE COCKTAIL AND PIZZA ORDERING LINE IS SUPER LONG, HEAD INSIDE AND ORDER YOUR PIZZA AND GLASS OF NATURAL WINE INSTEAD. THERE'S HARDLY EVER A WAIT, AND THEY FREQUENTLY HAVE LIVE JAZZ OR ANY LOCAL ON THE PIANO JUST FOR FUN.

6

DINO'S

Late-night eaters, this one's for you! East Nashville's most beloved and oldest dive bar is also home to one of the best burgers in town, and frequently acts as a post-show celebrity hot spot, so keep your eyes peeled! Located on the main road in East Nashville, DINO'S best represents all the good parts of this side of town. It's grungy, all about friends and community, and has some seriously good food. They even landed in the top three in Bon Appétit magazine rankings of the best burgers in the US in 2017. And you really can't argue with the low price point.

Dino's is a place your parents (or at least mine) love. It feels like the good ol' days, with its dim lights, dark wood, and plenty of tables and bar seats to gather with friends.

The staff cranks out burgers, fries, a Damn Sandwich (two slices of toasted white bread, bacon, egg, cheese, and special sauce), and every cheap beer you can imagine. They also have a special brunch menu on Saturday and Sunday, complete with hot chicken french toast drizzled with hot honey maple syrup, huevos rancheros, and a breakfast patty melt to make it all okay to have the famous cheeseburger for breakfast. Hang out on the patio with some friends and a beermosa alongside the Dolly Parton lemon stand. I know this may sound confusing, but there's really a giant lemon with a bar inside, and a Dolly figurine on top!

7

BUTCHER & BEE

The tastefully hip, Israeli-inspired brunch and dinner-time favorite is so unique to Nashville and checks a lot of boxes. You'll find the vibey outdoor patio; a very pretty bar; plant-forward, immaculate cocktails; and a whipped feta dip that literally became an overnight sensation, and is still famous. **BUTCHER & BEE** is great for big group dinners, date nights, or drinks with friends at the bar. The space is quite big and certainly always busy. You'll notice the open

Andrew Cebulka

kitchen, fresh produce in wooden crates displayed on the wall, and the very high ceilings. Whether you are looking for a non-basic brunch or a vibey date night, book a reservation and be ready to try something different!

As for the menu, I love digging into the shareable options. Curate your own mezze board or have the staff pick their personal favorites. Speaking to the non-basic brunch, the crispy rice is always a must, especially when it's served alongside collards, peanuts, serrano chilis, and avocado, with the optional shawarma chicken. Throughout the menu you can expect really bold, herby flavors—eastern ethnicities blended with some southern twang in perfect food harmony.

THE CLEVELAND PARK CRAWL

1. **MAS TACOS,** 732 MCFERRIN AVE., NASHVILLE, (615) 543-6271, HTTPS://WWW.INSTAGRAM.COM/MASTACOS

2. **PHARMACY BURGER PARLOR & BEER GARDEN,** 731 MCFERRIN AVE., NASHVILLE, (615) 712-9517, HTTPS://WWW.THEPHARMACYBURGER.COM

3. **REDHEADED STRANGER,** 305 ARRINGTON ST., NASHVILLE, (615) 544-8226, HTTPS://WWW.REDHEADEDSTRANGERTACOS.COM

4. **FOLK,** 823 MERIDIAN ST., NASHVILLE, (615) 610-2595, HTTPS://WWW.GOODASFOLK.COM

5. **LYRA,** 935 W. EASTLAND AVE., NASHVILLE, (615) 928-8040, HTTPS://WWW.LYRANASHVILLE.COM

6. **XIAO BAO,** 830 MERIDIAN ST, NASHVILLE, (615) 239-5553, HTTPS://WWW.XIAOBAONASHVILLE.COM

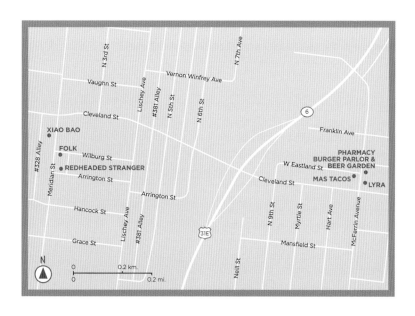

Cleveland Park

Around the World in One Neighborhood

This unassuming neighborhood has become a coveted spot. With its proximity to downtown, Germantown, and other parts of East Nashville, it became a natural place to locate small businesses. More recently it has become flooded with coffee shops and trendy new restaurants, both casual and high-end.

There are plenty of bungalows and a bit of Victorian influence among the homes, making for some very charming views. You'll find some of Nashville's best casual tacos right by one of my favorite fine dining options. There's no shortage of good meals and there's plenty of options.

1

MAS TACOS

This East Nashville establishment is one of the city's greatest treasures. The divey street taco restaurant has lived on the corner lot of an up-and-coming neighborhood since 2010. As I like to say, provide the tacos, and the people will come. Prior to 2010, MAS TACOS was a one-woman food truck and has earned its reputation as the tacos to have in Nashville, so expect a line out the door upon arrival! As you enter the building, be prepared to be immersed in a colorful, authentic, lively, magical taco land.

The menu is written on the chalkboard wall above the cash register and is often accompanied by a daily special. They also recently introduced an ordering window outside if you're looking to get your food to-go or have

your dog with you and want to head straight to their shaded patio. If you're lucky, you'll get there on a day they're serving their Pickled Cactus and Chorizo Taco! Off of their regular menu, I almost always go for the spicy Carne Molida Taco (Cuban-style ground beef, spicy onions, salsa, and sour cream) and the Fried Avocado Taco (shaved cabbage, onions, and spicy dill yogurt). Another must-have is the chicken tortilla soup—it's the perfect side, especially on a chilly day. And of course, no Mexican street food meal is complete without a side of elote, corn on the cob smothered in spicy cream sauce and fresh cheese, and horchata to drink! If you're feeling boozy, Mas Tacos doesn't cheat. All their drinks are ridiculously fresh, so try the classic margarita or ask about their specials.

Pharmacy Burger

2 PHARMACY BURGER PARLOR & BEER GARDEN

If the idea of house-made sausages, soda floats, a beef strogannoff burger, and adults drinking out of extra-large steins excites you, then head to **PHARMACY BURGER PARLOR & BEER GARDEN**, one of the dreamiest beer gardens, complete with its own little beer hut. Whether you're sitting outside or in, you will be surrounded by a European beer hall aesthetic. Hanging outdoors with twinkly lights at a picnic table with a stein in hand makes for a pretty perfect day. But don't get me wrong, this restaurant is super family-friendly! The long, German-styled tables make it easy to find a seat or dine with a big group for lunch and dinner.

The first time I went to Pharmacy Burger, I went for the beef stroganoff burger—mushroom stroganoff bechamel, sour cream, caramelized onions, and Swiss cheese nestled in a dense, pillowy bun (and kudos to them, they take the extra step of lightly toasting it, which makes all the difference). My other go-to, if you're not feeling a burger, is the Currywurst—a classic brat, poached, smoked, and then simmered with a light pilsner beer and topped with a curried paprika and tomato sauce. Pharmacy makes all their sausages in-house. I mean, they grind, stuff, and smoke every sausage in the kitchen, so you are getting the absolute best of the wurst! Each sausage and burger comes with your choice of side plus a list of more than ten sauces to choose from. It's hard to break the habit of always ordering the roasted garlic aioli, horseradish mustard, and curry ketchup! Pair your meal with a beer from their extensive imported list plus a house-made phosphate (it's like a dessert and soda all in one!). Trust their knowledgeable and friendly staff to guide you to the right choice. Prost!

Pharmacy Burger

3

REDHEADED STRANGER

REDHEADED STRANGER has created quite the buzz around town as it filled Nashville's need for a true Texan neighborhood taco shop. This place is just bursting with bright southwestern accents. The outside of the restaurant welcomes you with a pastel-painted cactus mural that makes for the perfect backdrop. Inside you'll find rainbow tile, light-pink retro diner chairs, cushy bar stools that spin, and walls lined with succulents. You just may want to move in!

One of the first things you'll notice when you walk in is the tortilla station right out in the open. The staff whips out fresh flour tortillas. Honestly, it's very impressive, it looks like it should be a sport. Along with the flour tortillas, I've learned a few tidbits that make this place a Texas taco joint. First thing is having a breakfast taco, one of their most popular being the Egg, Chorizo, Sour Cream, and Cheddar. The second thing is having a Texas staple–brisket, which you can find labeled as Taco #7 Brisket Taco on the

menu. It features chopped brisket, egg, American cheese, and my sauce of choice—the Dr. Pepper hot sauce, yet another necessary Texas delicacy. And, oh my, it is so dang delicious—sweet, spicy, and a little weird. Lucky for customers, additional hot sauces are self-serve, including Chef Weaver's original Dreamweaver hot sauce, so you're able to indulge in them all.

Lately my go-to has been the #6 Tater Tot Taco (tater tots, jalapeno crema, red hatch chilis, and American cheese). Putting tater tots in a taco was something I had never previously thought of, but now it's something I can't forget. Accompany it with Frito Pie (Texas red chili, cheddar cheese, sour cream, and pico de gallo loaded into a bag of Fritos—I mean how could you not, right?), and a Banana Pudding Shake spiked with bourbon, and you will walk away happy and very full.

4

FOLK

I find myself at **FOLK** time and time again, whether it's an hour before opening and my husband and I check to see if by chance there's an early spot available in the bar during the work week, or if we're reserving a 7:30 p.m. dinner slot on a Friday night. Folk's menu is always filled with creative shareables, one of the many reasons they became a semi-finalist for Best New Restaurant by the James Beard Foundation in 2019. Founded by Chef P.K. Rolf, also owner of Rolf and Daughters in the Germantown neighborhood, this restaurant

focuses on seasonal Italian small plates and upscale pizza. I find Folk to be the perfect balance of fancy and hip. Upon arrival you'll immediately notice the abundance of greenery, exposed brick in an intimate but open bar area, and a mighty fine looking wine wall where the staff will smartly help you pick the right grape for your taste buds.

Folk is renowned for their bread-making skills, so naturally an order of sourdough is the only proper way to begin your visit. Follow up with a plate of country ham if it's on rotation. Despite its name, this ham is a classy, thin cut from a local farm. The vegetables, seafood, and meat options change

with the seasons. Expect the best of the best ingredients—you'll see what I mean when you sample their Caesar salad with their ever-so-stunning greens, fluffy cheese, sourdough croutons, and fish roe. Make your way to the bottom of the menu and you'll find the pizza! I am so pleased to tell you they have a clam pizza with lemon, chili, bonito, and parsley. Clam pizza and I go way back in my childhood to a small pizza joint on Long Island where my family and I would frequently get takeout, so I'm a little biased. Being able to enjoy this funky pizza in Nashville—well, that's just really special. Eat your way through this shareable menu, and end on a sweet note with something along the lines of a tiramisu cream puff or some panna cotta, and if you're like me, an after-dinner coffee.

TIP

AFTER DINNER, HEAD TO THE WATERING HOLE AROUND THE COR- NER CALLED WILBURN STREET TAVERN. PLAY SOME POOL, DRINK SOMETHING CHEAP, AND STAY OUT FAR TOO LATE.

5

LYRA

LYRA is a modern Middle Eastern restaurant that is a go-to for happy hour, a drink at the bar, a romantic evening on the patio, or a private party in their back room. Instantly you'll smell the fresh pita and aromatic spices that inspire their dishes. Touches of teal and gold appear throughout the interior, and a greenery-filled outdoor area is jazzed up with string lights and nearby neighbors. Lyra is frequently switching up the menu, and their cheery staff is always happy to guide you through the unique dishes. I always find myself learning a thing or two about the Middle Eastern food culture when I go.

So maybe you've caught on to this by now, but my favorite after-work activity is drinking wine on a patio. Both my own and someone else's. If you're into shareables, twinkly lights, and the aforementioned fresh pita, Lyra is an incredible choice for all the fresh breads, dips, and then some. The man'oushe—a great deal at happy hour—is a warm, freshly baked flatbread covered in za'atar seasoning (traditionally made with a blend of thyme, oregano, sesame seeds, sumac, and salt). Lyra also offers a Hummus Collective (for those who can't make up their minds) and Pistachio Whipped Feta with fresh veggies. Another Middle Eastern classic is the Baba Ganoush, an eggplant-based dip filled with spices, lemon, and whichever drool-worthy way they want to spice it up that day. Moving to entrees, you'll find extremely rich and colorful dishes. I always find myself ordering the Seared Octopus or one of the lamb dishes. The main dishes are always paired with seasonal bright fruits like pomegranate, pickled vegetables, chickpeas, or a special rice. If you're into herbs, spices, and something quite different, this is your place!

6   XIAO BAO

I was so excited to hear that **XIAO BAO** was coming to Nashville. As a former Charleston summer bum, I fondly recall many meals and cocktails at the original laid-back location. The Nashville location has one of the most unique decor styles in the city. I don't know the full story here, but there's a strawberry structure in the front yard of the restaurant that's a little fruit house you can go inside just for fun. The fun continues as you enter the actual restaurant, with bright red shiny booths and cushioned stools, fun wallpaper, and a bit of a seventies feel.

The fun continues with the Asian comfort food menu. My favorite is the sake juice box with the biang biang hand-pulled noodles that come with their own set of scissors. The Som Tum is their spicy papaya salad—it's a favorite, but it is SPICY! It is spicier than most hot chickens in town, so if you're looking to test your taste buds, add this to the list! Their tidy and intentional cocktail list is injected with savory flavors, citrus, and more spice. Xiao Bao is open for lunch and dinner and has so many playful elements throughout. Stop in for a casual lunch; plan dinner here for an impressive first date; or rent out the private, metallic room in the back for some karaoke.

Xiao Bao

Xiao Bao

THE EASTWOOD AND INGLEWOOD CRAWL

1. **LOU,** 1304 MCGAVOCK PIKE, NASHVILLE, (615) 499-4495, HTTPS://WWW.LOUNASHVILLE.COM

2. **CAFE ROZE,** 1115 PORTER RD., NASHVILLE, (615) 645-9100, HTTPS://WWW.CAFEROZE.COM

3. **TWO TEN JACK,** 1900 EASTLAND AVE. #105, NASHVILLE, (615) 454-2731, HTTPS://WWW.TWOTENJACK.COM

4. **PEARL DIVER,** 1008 GALLATIN AVE., NASHVILLE, (615) 988-2265, HTTPS://WWW.PEARLDIVERNASHVILLE.COM

5. **ONCE UPON A TIME IN FRANCE,** 1102 GALLATIN AVE., NASHVILLE, (615) 649-8284, HTTPS://WWW.ONCEUPONATIME-INFRANCE.COM

6. **NOKO,** 701 PORTER RD., NASHVILLE, (615) 712-6894, HTTPS://WWW.NOKONASHVILLE.COM

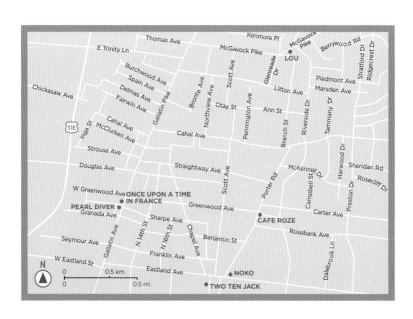

Eastwood and Inglewood

It's Hip, It's Delish, It's Local

Just ten or so minutes from downtown, you'll run into Eastwood and Inglewood, home to the Shops at Porter Road, a collection of shops, restaurants, and dessert places nestled in the neighborhood on Eastland Avenue. Follow a tree-lined road to the very quaint Riverside Village. Gallatin Avenue (the main road that runs through East) is scattered with thrift shops, dive bars, restaurants, music venues, a few pawn shops, and "cash now" types of places. You'll find some truly stunning homes, lush greenery, and lots of young parents and millennials walking about. But here you'll also find Nashville's best ramen, a restaurant inside a little white bungalow that I fell in love with before it opened, and a Cuban-inspired bar complete with pu pu platters and some raved-about cocktails.

1

LOU

LOU really satisfies the pieces of my soul and stomach that want to be both Parisian and a southerner. As someone who often daydreams about dropping everything and moving to France, I can get my fix at this California-French inspired restaurant and all natural wine bar that has truly filled a void in our food community. Inside an old craftsman house in Riverside Village, the atmosphere totally matches the warmth of the people who work there. Our very cool girl owner, Mailea Weger, is a Southern California native who began her career in the fashion industry, gave a farewell to that part of her life, went on to work at a restaurant in Paris, and (lucky for us) chose Nashville as the city in which to open Lou. It's not rare to see her hustling at her own restaurant, at various pop-ups and community events alike, putting on the annual charity bake sale, or even on a plane to France as she works on new projects in Paris!

For those who prefer to walk on the salty side at brunch, Lou almost always has a lima bean dish, which, I know, sounds a little rogue for the brunch hours, but it's consistently one of my favorites on the menu, alongside a buckwheat pancake, lox on anything, and a pastry, maybe two. I highly recommend making a reservation, but if you're lucky you might just be able to snag a walk-in seat at their four-person tiny bar!

Lou at dinnertime is chic and romantic, candle-lit, and makes you feel as if you're in on a really good secret. Build your own charcuterie board

with local meats and cheeses and other rotating specialty items such as eggs with black sesame-miso butter. For the table, the crispy rice is always on my rotation. For the entrees, you'll have the option to choose between land and sea. Lou does operate on a seasonal menu, but if there's skirt steak, anything with fermented chili yogurt, or a bucksnort trout, get it! Wind down with a dessert wine, ice cream, cake, and maybe a coffee. Merci, Lou, for being so special.

TIP

IN THE SUMMERTIME LOU HAS A MOVIE SERIES WHERE YOU CAN EAT DINNER AND THEY'LL PROJECT A MOVIE ON THEIR PATIO. I HIGHLY RECOMMEND CHECKING THEIR SCHEDULE ON THEIR SOCIAL MEDIA @ LOU_NASHVILLE TO SEE IF YOU CAN GET A SEAT!

2 CAFE ROZE

CAFE ROZE has really become part of my dining routine. I'll frequently post-up at the bar for oysters and dirty martinis and a much needed catch-up with a good friend. The posh but low-key environment has a way of keeping you into the evening. The long and narrow space makes you feel as if you're tucked away somewhere along a city street, when really you're in the center of a bungalow-filled neighborhood. The bar stretches along the right side of the space while tables line the left. The exposed ceilings and cement floors

are complemented by soft pinks and natural wood. It's very cozy and you'll likely get to know your neighbor over a bit of banter between meals.

The cafe is open from 8:00 a.m. to 10:00 p.m., with daytime (8:00 a.m. to 3:30 p.m.), "In Between" (3:30 to 4:00 p.m.), happy hour (4:00 to 6:00 p.m.), and dinner (4:00 to 10 p.m.) menus. Every dish is beaming with natural colors, and the drinks are chic and non-fussy. A memorable cocktail I've had here in the past is the Shelby Park Swizz, with Fidencio Mezcal, Génépy, St. Germain, and pineapple. If you're there for brunch but not quite ready to get a buzz, I recommend the Turmeric Cooler (spiced turmeric blend with lemon and sparkling water). This effervescent beverage will get you ready to take on the day in no time.

If you find yourself struggling on what to eat for brunch, may I suggest their signature Roze Bowl, a delicious (and healthy) choice featuring beet tahini, black lentils, red quinoa, a seasonal vegetable, kale, and pickled beets. I'm not one to avoid seafood for breakfast either, so if that's your motto as well, then go on and get the Smoked Trout Toast, topped with a bed of radishes for a perfect crunch, lemon, and chives.

For dinner, you may be surprised to hear that the eggplant is by far my favorite. I've never imagined a seemingly old-school vegetable could be reinvented in this way. This chili and quinoa–coated eggplant topped with salsa negra, fresh herbs and microgreens, and charred orange vinaigrette easily makes this one of my top meals in Nashville.

3

TWO TEN JACK

Ramen probably isn't the first cuisine you think of when in the South, but TWO TEN JACK has become a must-visit whenever friends come to town or whenever we're just craving really great, feel-good food. Upon arrival, make your way to the very end of the courtyard filled with a local coffee shop, bakery, and a few fun stores and find the glowing red light. Two Ten is Nashville's first izakaya, most famously known for their big slurpy bowls of ramen. They truly value the quality of their food and the state in which it's served. For that reason, you cannot take your ramen to go! And for that reason, I highly recommend making a reservation.

You can expect a relaxed patio filled with locals aplenty, community tables, a wrap-around bar, intimate booths, and soundless animae projected on the wall for your enjoyment. While the ramen is the most popular, the rest of the menu is filled with fun appetizers, fresh fish, noodles, and more. The Takoyaki, or as we describe it, an octopus hush puppy, comes with a side of miso butter for dipping and is one of my top bites in town. I recommend trying out a few of the yakitori (tiny skewers of meat or vegetables, usually grilled). I typically order pork belly, skirt steak, and cherry

tomato; they're perfect to share and a fun way to try a little of everything. Be sure to pair your experience with one of Two Ten Jack's unique cock-tails and end with a Strawberry and Green Tea Mochi, a sweet and frozen Japanese rice cake filled with ice cream.

4 PEARL DIVER

The first time I stumbled into **PEARL DIVER**, I wasn't looking for Havana in Nashville, but I found it! This mid-century, tropical space is one of my top, aesthetically pleasing bars in Nashville. Pearl Diver really stands out from the rest of the crowd, outside and in. The Palm Springs–like architecture and porthole windows make you feel as if you're anywhere but the middle of the south. On a nice evening, make your way out to the courtyard in the back. For big parties, you can reserve a green leather booth or cabana on the patio. The retro-nautical-Cuban influences bring an original concept to the city.

The bartenders are super talented when it comes to crafting signature drinks that have just the right amount of freshness, island influence, and buzz. There's a long list of rum cocktails, including the Yum Yum made with dark rum, coconut cream, lemongrass, Thai basil, Thai chili, and fresh lime. For food, the Pastor tacos with pineapple are always a go-to, or you can share their PuPu Platter complete with egg rolls, dumplings, Hawaiian meatballs, chicken wings, mini gringo tacos, beef bulgogi, and grilled pineapple skewers on a spinning platter.

5 ONCE UPON A TIME IN FRANCE

This no-res, warm 1920s inspired French bistro is as authentic as it gets. Yes, the owners are from France, and they tend to hire French-speaking staff. Hearing the banter between them over a red table wine, escargot, and vintage oddities could entirely convince you you're across the pond. This seemingly divey building turns out some very cozy, traditional dishes.

The menu at **ONCE UPON A TIME IN FRANCE** is petite and consistent, six hors d'oeuvres, five entrees, and three desserts. For the adventurous: garlic and parsley butter escargot, beef tartare, duck and chicken country pate, and duck foie gras. On the entree side, I can't leave anywhere without trying the duck. The Confit de Canard comes with roasted potatoes, reduced duck sauce, and a small side of greens. Other French classics include steak frites, coq au vin, and a gorge trout filet. After dinner, espresso and a chocolate mousse are an absolute must!

6 NOKO

NOKO opened in March 2023 as one of the most talked about new restaurants, and for very good reason. The Japanese farmhouse aesthetic is clean minimalism meets warm and homey, just like the food—and the staff for that matter! Noko is one of those great places that is very intentional about creating a sustainable work environment in the hospitality industry, and it totally shows.

The menu consists of fresh fish, wood-fire cooking, and rich and savory small plates. Everything was inspired by the founder's extensive travel experience, with heavy Asian influences and non-traditional flavors that blend delightfully well, like a burrata made with tomato and Thai basil pesto.

I can never turn down a Tuna Crispy Rice, especially a spicy one with serrano peppers and a little sweetness along with a Hamachi tuna. Another super fun dish was the Wagyu Tartare where you are given toasted nori (seaweed), sticky rice, and a small wooden spoon to create your very own hand rolls. One more meaty bite from left field was the Bone Marrow accompanied by toasted baguettes and wood-fired chimichurri. Still, perhaps the most talked about menu item is the Dole Whip—a frozen fruit ice cream of sorts, reminiscent of the kind received at Disney—tart, creamy, and a little whimsical.

Addison Leboutillier

THE GERMANTOWN CRAWL

1. **HENRIETTA RED,** 1200 4TH AVE. N., NASHVILLE, (615) 490-8042, HTTPS://WWW.HENRIETTARED.COM

2. **ROLF AND DAUGHTERS,** 700 TAYLOR ST., NASHVILLE, (615) 866-9897, HTTPS://WWW.ROLFANDDAUGHTERS.COM

3. **STEAM BOYS,** 1200 2ND AVE. N., NASHVILLE, (615) 678-6336, HTTPS://WWW.STEAMBOYS.COM

4. **CITY HOUSE,** 1222 4TH AVE. N., NASHVILLE, (615) 736-5838, HTTPS://WWW.CITYHOUSENASHVILLE.COM

5. **SLIM & HUSKY'S,** 911 BUCHANAN ST., NASHVILLE, (615) 561-1787, HTTPS://WWW.SLIMANDHUSKYS.COM

6. **BUTCHERTOWN HALL,** 1416 4TH AVE. N., NASHVILLE, (615) 454-3634, HTTPS://WWW.BUTCHERTOWNHALL.COM

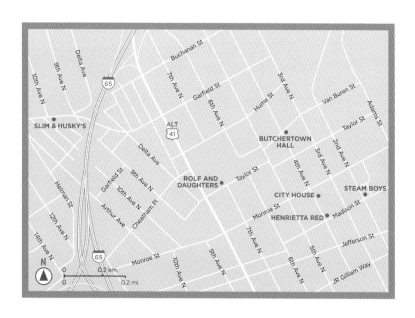

Germantown

Charming Streets and Fancy Dinners

I proclaim Germantown one of Nashville's cutest neighborhoods. It still has a few cobblestone roads, shady streets, and historic homes. The quiet nature of this area makes it a sought-after place to live. Along with that, it seems to be a hub of romantic dining destinations, within walking distance of our minor league baseball stadium, home to galleries and art collectives, boasts a riverside walking trail, and offers a brewery or two. As you may be able to assume by its name, this neighborhood hosts Oktoberfest filled with wiener dog races, lots of hot fancy dogs, and steins for all. The area is rich in history. In the 1850s it was the first Nashville suburb, filled with European immigrants and all their influences. Germantown is also home to the Nashville Farmers' Market, full of restaurants in the interior, and local farmers set up under the covered exterior, mixed in with a little retail therapy for a perfect Nashville souvenir.

1

HENRIETTA RED

HENRIETTA RED is Nashville's temporary escape to the ocean. Its interior is bright and airy; filled with lounge seating, community tables, coastal inspiration, and Nashville's most notable raw bar. This space is nothing short of perfection. Power duo Chef Julia Sullivan and Sommelier Allie Poindexter met while working in New York, and then set off to Nashville, Julia's hometown, opening Henrietta in 2017 on their quaint street in Germantown.

You can't walk into Henrietta Red and not feel inspired to get oysters! Choose from their à la carte raw menu or go for the wood-roasted oysters with Calabrian chili and sourdough breadcrumbs. What I admire most about the menu is the abundance of citrus flavors, which, when combined with the fresh seafood dishes and vibrant vegetables, make these dishes oh so sprightly and full of joy. Perhaps the most stunning dish I've had there is the smoked trout toast featured on their brunch menu, topped with labna (a creamy cheese made from strained yogurt), capers, roasted cabbage, mesmerizingly beautiful purple radishes, and dill. Don't shy away from the crab cake atop rich, green butter lettuce with grapefruit, and a lemon aioli, or a seasonal polenta with mushroom, pesto, chopped almonds, poached eggs, and a fresh fluffy blanket of parmesan. Not a seafood lover? No worries—the burger is for everyone made with fontal cheese, whole grain mustard aioli for a little kick, and a brioche bun.

Find their dinner menu filled with the same plentifulness of citrus and herbs, served with seasonal items such as red snapper, mushroom steak, duck breast, and even chicken liver. Pair your experience with their natural wines or their cava (Spanish sparkling wine). Be sure to pick out a sweet for yourself off their dessert menu, and you'll be leaving with a full heart (and stomach).

2

ROLF AND DAUGHTERS

If someone invites you to **ROLF AND DAUGHTERS**, don't think, just go ! Enter through their herb garden under string lights, and a black and white mural of curious human faces. I'm fairly positive this restaurant invented the chic warehouse look, then took it up a notch by offering seasonal dishes with an emphasis on fresh pasta and unorthodox vegetable-heavy plates. One time I went and every one of their cocktails was named after a bad haircut. So would you like a Toupée or a Bowl Cut? Whichever your style preference (the wine list is quite somethin' as well), the atmosphere is ideal for a lively dinner.

A small tidbit: Rolf and Daughters has a younger sister restaurant, Folk, over in East Nashville. Both are known for their house-made sourdough bread. At Rolf, it's typically served with their seaweed butter, which is always a nice little surprise. Since their menu can change daily, it would be a little rude of me to tease you with what might be on there the time you go. But, believe me, everything is delicately ramped with flavor. And if pasta is your soulmate, Rolf and Daughters is the place for you.

3 STEAM BOYS

If you didn't already find Chinese food a comfort, just wait until you take out some **STEAM BOYS**. This fast casual restaurant not only feeds your soul with warm delicious happiness, but it's also a fresh, healthy, traditional menu that brings authentic bao, dumplings, noodle soups, and more. Stay for a quick bite, linger over lunch, or take home an order or two of dumplings for an evening on the couch with a movie. Whether you want a snack, a full meal, or a boba tea, you have all of the options here.

Whether you are a carnivore or a vegan, Steam Boys has you covered. Start off with one, big and beautiful, juicy Pork Bao filled with their signature style pork, ginger, cabbage, and green onions, or try the Veggie Bao with napa cabbage, mushrooms, carrots, peas, and rice noodles, both wrapped in airy dough. And if you're really looking for that rainy day satisfaction, look no further than the noodle soups to slurp you into a comfy night. I recommend the Beef Noodle Soup and their seared bao buns. The extra crisp gives a beautiful texture to the already phenomenal flavors within.

5 SLIM & HUSKY'S

Y'all. Get Ready. Because this pizza joint is going to take over the world! Their motto is "PREAM" aka, Pizza Rules Everything Around Me. They scream PREAM, they live PREAM. Just a short ride outside Germantown in the Buchanan Arts District, you'll happen upon this build-your-own pizza joint blasting hip-hop, welcoming in all the folks, and firing out pies faster than you can order off the menu.

There are many reasons I enjoy **SLIM & HUSKY'S**: the inclusive nature, the music, the fact that corn is offered as a topping, but mostly it's just good pizza with lots of options. What I love about this build-your-own pizza are the inventive drizzles and dipping sauces, including balsamic molasses or jalapeno cilantro ranch for all your crusts. Post pizza, get yourself a famous cinnamon roll, such as the Ninja Tartle with green apple sauce and jalapeno cream cheese, or the Halle Berry with blueberry sauce and fresh lemon glaze.

6 BUTCHERTOWN HALL

This Tex-Mex-inspired BBQ and craft taco restaurant is all things cacti, brisket, pineapple margaritas, and anything they can woodfire. Enter through a large, sunny patio into the sub-way-tiled, plant-filled dining area. The restaurant itself is mas-sive, with extra tall ceilings and large windows that flood in light. The atmosphere makes for the perfect brunch, group dinner, or simply a drink at the bar.

Just a 411, **BUTCHERTOWN HALL** may have one of the best queso and guac in Nashville, and you probably didn't hear it here first. The classic double patty burger on a brioche bun with a side of brussels sprouts is super popular. You're also able to order meat by the pound with ribs, pork loins, brisket, and other Texan delicacies (though might I suggest you plan for a nap after). For those into upscale tacos, I recommend the Fire-Roasted Shrimp with charred cabbage and avocado crema.

THE DOWNTOWN CRAWL

1. **ACME FEED & SEED,** 101 BROADWAY, NASHVILLE, (615) 915-0888, HTTPS://WWW.ACMEFEEDANDSEED.COM

2. **ROBERT'S WESTERN WORLD,** 416 BROADWAY #B, NASHVILLE, (615) 244-9552, HTTPS://WWW.ROBERTSWESTERNWORLD.COM

3. **SKULL'S RAINBOW ROOM,** 222 PRINTER'S ALLEY, NASHVILLE, (615) 810-9631, HTTPS://WWW.SKULLSRAINBOWROOM.COM

4. **PINEWOOD SOCIAL,** 33 PEABODY ST., NASHVILLE, (615) 751-8111, HTTPS://WWW.PINEWOODSOCIAL.COM

5. **MARTIN'S BAR-B-QUE JOINT,** 410 4TH AVE. S., NASHVILLE, (615) 288-0880, HTTPS://WWW.MARTINSBBQJOINT.COM

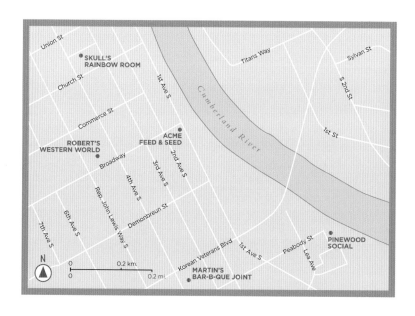

Downtown

Get Your Honky-Tonk On

It's what most people come for. Downtown Nashville, most known for Broadway: home to honky tonks, bachelorette parties, CMA Fest, live music at every entry, and wild, wild times. Before these four-story buildings with rooftops were bars, they were occupied by all sorts of businesses, such as farm supply stores, guitar manufacturers, and speakeasies. While downtown isn't typically where locals go most frequently (at least after living here for a while), it can definitely be a rowdy and fun time with the right crowd. Explore all the side streets, the main streets, and take in the bright lights and sounds of music city.

1

ACME FEED & SEED

This four-story Broadway bar and restaurant is here for all your live music, rooftop river views, casual eats, and party time. The building was originally constructed in 1890 and was home to many businesses in the early days, the longest standing being Acme Farm Supply, known for hosting many memorable family-friendly events. They owned a famous pet calf named Beautena who appeared on stage at the Grand Ole Opry during commercial breaks. The reason I tell you this is because the rich history of the building is honored throughout the space, giving you a taste of the Nashville scene, past and present.

As you enter the first floor of **ACME FEED & SEED**, you can be greeted by anything from acoustic pop to bluegrass on any given day. The ground-floor menu features some southern classics with a little flare, including Rule the Roost (hot chicken with green peppercorn aioli) and Beer Belly Tacos, but my personal favorite is their sushi bar on the second floor. Enjoy a Sushi Boat with ten of your closest friends (hello, girls' trip), relax on their vintage lounge seats, or play a little shuffleboard while you wait for

APPETIZERS & SALADS
MISO SOUP - 4
GINGER SALAD - 5
EDAMAME - 6
PORK GYOZA - 7
EGG ROLLS - 6
SHRIMP TEMPURA - 10
FRIED SOFT SHELL CRAB - 7
CALAMARI - 7
TUNA TATAKI - 9
seared tuna, served with ponzu sauce

SPECIALTY PLAT
BENTO
Orange chicken, pork
Choice of mis...

SUSHI B
Red Dragon, Godzilla, and C...
Chef's choice Nigiri a...

MAKI ROLLS
CUCUMBER ROLL - 5
AVOCADO ROLL - 6
SALMON ROLL - 7
TUNA ROLL - 7
YELLOWTAIL ROLL - 7

NIGIRI AND SASHIMI
AVAILABLE BY REQUEST
... poultry, seafood, shellfish,
...orne illnesses

your food. Head up to the fourth-floor rooftop, and you get a five-star view of Nashville's Cumberland River and the Nissan Titan's Stadium. The rooftop is known for their Mule Kicker (aka moonshine lemonade slushy) that will, yes, kick you one way or another. Sip up top and people-watch the infamous street that is Broadway, and don't forget to stop in the Acme Farm Store on the way out. It'll have some of the best souvenirs you can find downtown!

2 ROBERT'S WESTERN WORLD

Take yourself back to the days of Willie Nelson, Loretta Lynn, and Hank Williams as you two-step your way into **ROBERT'S WESTERN WORLD**. From the late 1950s to the early 1980s, this building was the home of Sho-Bud Steel Guitar Company, making the best of the kind for many legends in the heyday of country music. There are truly not many places left that play the old-school jigs of yesteryear, which is what makes Robert's so unique to Broadway. If the soulful southern tunes from years past don't fully convince you that you've gone back in time, then the $2.50 beer will definitely have you believing. Admire those around you who are there for the music, and take a peek at the boot shelves and photo wall of celebrities who have made some good memories on the stage.

You have until about 2:30 a.m. on any given night to get yourself one of the best burgers in Nashville. The open grill right behind the bar steams up some quality late-night eats. No judgment on all of you staying out until the late hours of the night—you're in Nashville, after all. After a night on Broadway, a fried bologna sandwich or burger with mushrooms and swiss is just what you need for a second dinner. Late night does get a bit crowded as you can imagine, but you can always catch the same good music, country dancing, and burgers during the daylight hours, which is what I prefer!

3

SKULL'S RAINBOW ROOM

The history behind **SKULL'S RAINBOW ROOM** is something that should be made into a film. Skull's is located on Printer's Alley, an almost European-feeling, cobblestone, no-car narrow path, with balconies and string lights illuminating the way for patrons to stumble into these unassuming bars. This area was one of the most popular during prohibition and actually has catacombs that run beneath to the Cumberland River (or so they say). The first time I ever went to Skull's Rainbow Room, I immediately felt as if I had time-hopped back into the 1920s. The black and white checkered tile, the stand-up bass and baby grand piano, the charming list of cocktails, and the fact that when you look around the room, no one is on their phone all sets the mood for an unforgettable evening.

The dinner menu perfectly complements your surroundings. I have a personal rule that if there's escargot on the menu, it's being ordered—likely alongside the bleu cheese wedge salad, foie gras, and Low Country Shrimp Cocktail. The main event on the dinner menu is the steaks, and the add-ons are very enticing. There's truly something beautiful in knowing I can add a lobster tail to my filet mignon, a dirty martini, and chocolate mousse cake for dessert while enjoying my favorite kind of jazzy music. It really feels like a French-American dream.

THE GULCH CRAWL

1. **PEG LEG PORKER BBQ,** 903 GLEAVES ST., NASHVILLE, (615) 829-6023, HTTPS://WWW.PEGLEGPORKER.COM

2. **TENNESSEE BREW WORKS,** 809 EWING AVE., NASHVILLE, (615) 436-0050, HTTPS://WWW.TNBREW.COM

3. **L. A. JACKSON AT THE THOMPSON HOTEL,** 401 11TH AVE. S., NASHVILLE, (615) 262-6007, HTTPS://WWW.LAJACKSONBAR.COM

4. **BISCUIT LOVE,** 316 11TH AVE. S., NASHVILLE, (615) 490-9584, HTTPS://WWW.BISCUITLOVE.COM

5. **ADELE'S,** 1210 MCGAVOCK ST., NASHVILLE, (615) 988-9700, HTTPS://WWW.ADELESRESTAURANT.COM

6. **EASTERN PEAK,** 133 12TH AVE. N., NASHVILLE, (615) 674-1411, HTTPS://WWW.THEEASTERNPEAK.COM

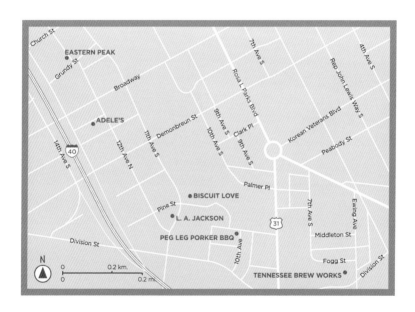

The Gulch

An Urban Neighborhood with Hidden Gems

Just down the road from the heart of downtown is the Gulch. This area is quite posh, which contradicts its history as a former railroad yard. But don't worry, there's still of lot of grit and train tracks and a few hidden, down-to-earth gems from the past scattered throughout. Today you'll find plenty of high-rise apartments, familiar shopping, and likely a very long line outside of Nashville's most popular destination for biscuits. The walkability of the neighborhood makes it a very desirable place to live, and a magnet for young professionals. The Gulch is filled with lively restaurants perfect for large groups, elevated cocktails on rooftops, and my favorite hot chicken sandwich.

1

PEG LEG PORKER BBQ

Past all the gentrification on the backside of the Gulch, follow the sweet smokey aroma to **PEG LEG PORKER BBQ**. This place is as real as it gets. Prior to opening Peg Leg in 2013, Pitmaster Carey Bringle actively participated in barbecue competitions for thirty years! Bringle grew up on West Tennessee que, with his grandfather blazing the trail of cooking hogs for friends and neighbors. It seems the pig doesn't run far from the pen, as Pitmaster Carey is all about family. Memorabilia lines the walls and shows just what kind of humble business he runs.

Before you even get inside, you'll notice a glass smoker where you can see exactly what they're firing up for the people. They call this the "aquarium smoker," and it's pretty darn cool. Welcome yourself inside and find the menu set up on a yellow letterboard. Cole slaw, mac and cheese, potato salad, and all the southern sides. I suggest bringing along a few friends so you can experience everything, including BBQ Nachos, Memphis Sushi (a sausage, cheese and saltine cracker platter), Kool-Aid Pickles (don't knock them 'till you try them), pork rinds, and, of course, a rack of dry ribs. That should just about cover it . . . for now. Head upstairs to the rooftop, better known as the Pig Pen, and grab yourself some of their specialty bourbon.

Peg Leg Porker

Peg Leg Porker

Before you leave, make sure you pick up some of Peg Leg's own dry rub, barbecue sauces, and merch! You can also head around the corner and find a pretty special chicken wing mural. I won't spoil the surprise completely—you'll just have to go see for yourself!

2 TENNESSEE BREW WORKS

It's not often you find a brewery where both the food and the beer are, well, amazing. While they might be located just outside of what people consider the Gulch, they stand on the cool, edgy side of the neighborhood where the breweries live. **TENNESSEE BREW WORKS**, or what I like to call TBW was one of the first places I was introduced to upon moving to Nashville, and I think I went there six times within two weeks. The food is phenomenal, upscale bar food; they have live music, two stories of indoor and outdoor space, and the beer list is the perfect balance of good classic styles, nature-driven subtle flavors, and a few adventurous blends. Plus, they have more than enough board games to keep everyone happy. So, if you're not already on your way, go, go, go!

A fun fact about TBW is that they make their food with their beer. Even their ketchup is made from their Basil Ryeman, a saison that's almost always sold out. It was so exceptionally good that I had an out-of-towner request a bottle so he could bring it back home. They complied, graciously. If you're

in town for some hot chicken, look no further. The juicy-to-crispiness ratio is unrivaled. It's topped with Extra Easy (malt beer) cheese and Cutaway (IPA) pickles. Served with a side of seasoned shoestring fries. Don't leave without splitting one of their artisanal cheese boards with some friends and an order of their Baja Fish Tacos, made with their State Park Blonde beer batter and miso glaze and served with their cabbage slaw.

3 L. A. JACKSON AT THE THOMPSON HOTEL

In search of Nashville's best view? Well, here it is! **L. A. JACKSON**, the rooftop bar at the Thompson Hotel, started off with a bang when it first opened in 2016, and the hype hasn't died down since. Walk into the lobby of the hotel and head straight back to the golden elevators.

If I were to describe L. A. Jackson in one word, it would be swanky. The indoor/outdoor rooftop is accented with leather, gold seats, a botanical mural, and chandeliers. There's also a live tree growing on the outside portion that's twinkled with fairy lights, and it makes sitting at this bar oh so magical. If you're in the mood for champagne, frosé, or one massive, beautiful presentation filled with Pickers Vodka, Génépy, strawberry, cucumber, lime, salt, and soda that they like to call The People's Choice, just know it requires a minimum of six people to order, so grab your squad and make your way to L. A. Jackson.

If you're dining in the warmer months, treat yourself to their brunch menu and DJ set while you take in the views. Their upscale but approachable menu will have lighter fare, such as freshly made french toast, seasonal fruit, and a lox bagel decorated with flowers, as well as their double patty burger and truffle fries with aioli. Start your evening at L. A. Jackson with a craft cocktail and a few bites off their bar snacks menu, and you have just begun your glamorous evening in Nashville.

4

BISCUIT LOVE

In 2012 owners Karl and Sarah Worley pooled all their money to start their Airstream food truck. Safe to say, it was a smart business decision. In 2015, the couple opened their first brick and mortar. **BISCUIT LOVE** holds the hearts of many across the nation due to their astounding customer service, southern hospitality, and—you guessed it—some really good biscuits. You'll never forget your first: flakey, buttery, fluffy perfection.

Biscuit Love is almost always crowded, but they keep the line moving and the biscuits flowing! Inside you'll be greeted by their extra-friendly staff and continue to experience that southern hospitality throughout your meal. As you may be able to infer by the name, Biscuit Love is all about the brunch. One of their most famous bites is the donut-biscuit hybrid, aka the Bonut! Fried biscuit dough coated in sugar, topped with lemon mascarpone on a bed of blueberry compote. Get an order of five of these little cuties and share them with the table. Or keep them all to yourself—I wouldn't blame you. Another equally fun dish is the Gertie, named after the owner's daughter who made this one up all on her own. It's a wonderful concoction of buttermilk biscuits, smothered in chocolate gravy, peanut butter, caramelized banana jam, and pretzel crunch. Moving toward the spicy side, try Biscuit Love's secret off-menu item, the Nasty Princess. A combination of the Princess and the East Nasty, this dish consists of a buttermilk biscuit sandwich topped with Nashville-style spicy boneless hot chicken coated in sausage gravy. Add a fried egg for extra fun.

While the Gulch location of Biscuit Love is the original, there are two more locations near and a little farther out! Visit them in their historic home in the heart of downtown Franklin, or at Gluten Alley in Hillsboro Village. Fun fact about the Hillsboro restaurant: Many years ago, this location was a bar where Sarah and Karl had their very first date. Once the building went up for sale, they knew it was destined to be their second location. Now that, my friends, is some Biscuit Love.

5 ADELE'S

I absolutely love going to **ADELE'S** for special occasions, especially with a big group! The indoor-outdoor, semi-industrial vibe is sprinkled with the most perfect color turquoise, features glass garage doors, and is full of natural light and city views. Nestled in the Gulch, Adele's gives you all the urban feels of Nashville with all the chicness of a stand-up Music City restaurant. Definitely a destination to keep on your rotation.

I love Adele's because it's so classic. You want a pork loin? New York strip? Rack of lamb? You got it. They're specifically known for their Salsa Verde Roasted Chicken. When I first had it, I didn't know a roasted chicken could taste that good. Whiskey and bourbon lovers will be right at home with their extensive local collection, and that right there is a nod to all the dads visiting in town.

6 EASTERN PEAK

Say it with me. Spicy cocktails. Noodles galore. Dramatic sushi. **EASTERN PEAK** has four locations in Nashville, which is no surprise because everything they do is excellent. At the Gulch location, you get all the city feels when you walk into the space. To the left, the large wraparound bar and lounge seating are ideal for a date (a first date at that), or five o'clock drinks and sushi with your favorite coworker. I would definitely recommend Eastern Peak for birthdays, bachelorettes, or anyone looking for an energetic dinner out.

For appetizers, I love the Crab Rangoon (little crab bites with cream cheese, crispy wontons, and sweet and sour sauce) and the Calamari Salt & Pepper (lightly breaded and fried, sooo deliciously peppery, mixed with garlic, onions, and peppers). The menu has a large variety of Asian cuisine, including a Thai favorite Pad Thai, various curries, fried rice, stir fry, and, of course, sushi. Get your classic rolls or get crazy with a signature special.

THE 12 SOUTH CRAWL

1. **BURGER UP,** 2901 12TH AVE. S., NASHVILLE, (615) 279-3767, HTTPS://WWW.BURGER-UP.COM

2. **FROTHY MONKEY,** 2509 12TH AVE. S., NASHVILLE, (615) 600-4756, HTTPS://WWW.FROTHYMONKEY.COM

3. **FIVE DAUGHTERS BAKERY,** 1110 CARUTHERS AVE., NASHVILLE, (615) 490-6554, HTTPS://WWW.FIVEDAUGHTERSBAKERY.COM

4. **CAFE MA'KAI,** 1210 WEDGEWOOD, AVE., NASHVILLE, (615) 823-3292, HTTPS://WWW.CAFEMAKAI.COM

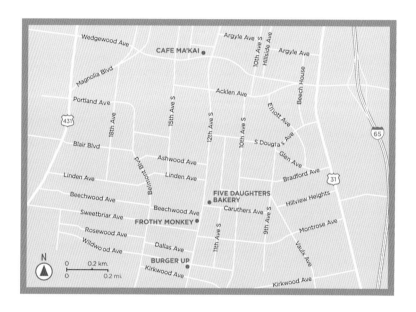

12 South

Brunch, Boutiques, and Photo Ops

Home to the original "I Believe In Nashville" mural, 12 South has become a bustling destination for visitors. It's filled with restaurants, coffee shops, bakeries, and lots of high-end boutiques for those who feel like having a fun shopping day. The heart of 12 South is the one long walkable street, 12th Avenue South. In the summer, you'll find the flower market right in the center—it'll transition into pumpkin-land for fall, and naturally, a Christmas tree market in December. This area is full of photo opportunities, adorable Airbnbs for parties big and small, and plenty of brunch spots. I can confidently say this is my mom's favorite place to frolic when she comes to visit, and for good reason! Start your morning at Frothy Monkey and make your way down the block to explore all 12 South has to offer.

1

BURGER UP

Welcome to the coziest of burger spots, **BURGER UP**! If you're looking to satisfy your patty craving but still want a nice cocktail and a variety of options, get yourself here! This sweet little spot is warm, lively, and has a bite for everyone. Because of its smaller nature and great food, expect a little bit of a wait

at peak hours! Since opening in 2010, Burger Up's mission has been to source locally and sustainably. Tennessee is extremely fortunate to have an abundance of farms to give our restaurants the best of the best to work with, and you can absolutely taste all that goodness in any burger you choose.

Don't skip out on the appetizers, friends! Especially when there are Fry Flights with a trio of dipping sauces, Fried Vidalia Onion Tower, and Mac and Cheese Bites. If you walk on the greener side of eating, I don't think I could ever talk about Burger Up without mentioning their Chopped Kale Salad, nor could anyone who has ever had it. Chopped curly green kale, roasted hazelnuts, dried tart cherries, pecorino Romano, with citrus vinaigrette. On the burger side, I love the French Onion Burger, which is loaded with arugula, fried onions, brie cheese, truffle aioli, caramelized onions and served on an onion roll. Upgrade your side to the truffle fries and be sure to dip in the homemade sauces set out on the table.

2 FROTHY MONKEY

Let's get you some coffee! And I'm not talking about your average cup of Joe, because **FROTHY MONKEY** has some of the best. In the heart of 12 South, you'll often see a line out the door of neighbors chatting in the front yard of this blue bungalow, many with their dogs in tow. This location is the original of the now six locations throughout the Nashville area and Chattanooga. Frothy Monkey prides itself on the farms they work with from all over the world and their ability to bring our community together through their locally roasted coffee.

Alongside their outstanding roasts is their equally cozy food. I'm talking biscuits and gravy; whole grain pancakes; and their Farm Breakfast, consisting of two farm eggs, pork sausage, herb-roasted red potatoes, orange wedges, and toast. Are you starting to pick up why this place is just all-around cozy? Their brunch menu is complete with Bloody Marys, mimosas, and Irish coffees! There's something really special about a coffee shop that can make you feel like you're part of the community, and that's Frothy.

Let's not forget to mention that they serve dinner . . . and wine! Let your soul be filled with their Chicken and Gnocchi, herb-marinated chicken breast with potato gnocchi, mushrooms, and spinach with pesto cream, or their Red Wine Braised Brisket, Wagyu brisket with wild mushroom ravioli, sweet green peas, onions, and herbed butter—all for a great price, might I add! Join them for "Wine Down Wednesday" at any location for by the glass and entree specials all night long.

3

FIVE DAUGHTERS BAKERY

First thing's first: Yes, there are actually five daughters! Owners Isaac and Stephanie Meek started their bakery in 2015 as a family affair with the launch of their 100-layer donut. Just off the main strip of 12 South, you'll find a little white house with bright turquoise and pink accents. There's a few tables inside and a patio area outside to enjoy. **FIVE DAUGHTERS BAKERY**'s 100-layer donuts are croissant-meets-donut magical bakery items that take a whole three days to prepare and are made with grass-fed butter, organic flour, and some very creative flavors. The result is a light, flakey, gone to heaven and back, melts in your mouth, type of donut.

If I had to pick a top flavor, it would be the King Kong, flavored with maple and topped with locally sourced bacon. Other flavors feature Vanilla Cream, Milk Chocolate Sprinkles, and a Chocolate Sea Salt. And, I don't mean to tease you, but some of their seasonal flavors have been Tiramisu (drool), Snickerdoodle, and Fluffernutter. Stop by this Nashville staple and grab a box to go. You can even see just how busy they are by watching the Donut Cam on their website!

4 CAFE MA'KAI

CAFE MA'KAI stole my heart the moment I walked in. I would describe the interior is a minimalistic, tropical cafe, with lots of warm wood. This peaceful eatery is filled with healthy options and is extremely vegan/vegetarian/gluten-free friendly. Co-owners Rowan Miller and Susan Richardson are also the owners of The Old School Farm to Table, located on a nine-acre farm just ten minutes outside of downtown where they grow produce, host events, and run their sustainably sourced restaurant.

Order your coffee and meal at the counter and shop their selection of locally made products. And, fun fact, all of the greenery is also available for purchase! Bring yourself home a surprise plant after lunch. But back to the food—one of my go-to favorites has been the Ham Toast: country ham on sourdough with grainy mustard, herbs, and pickled veggies. Of course, you can't go wrong with the Avocado Toast, topped with pickled onions (can you tell that I have a thing for all things vinegary yet?), cilantro, chilis, and edible flower petals. Hang out for a while, and you can grab yourself a cocktail at the bar.

THE BERRY HILL AND 8TH AVENUE CRAWL

1. **VUI'S KITCHEN,** 2832 BRANSFORD AVE., NASHVILLE, (615) 241-8847, HTTPS://WWW.VUISKITCHEN.COM

2. **BAJA BURRITO,** 722 THOMPSON LN., NASHVILLE, (615) 383-2252, HTTP://BAJABURRITO.COM

3. **THE SMILING ELEPHANT,** 2213 8TH AVE. S., (615) 891-4488, HTTPS://WWW.THESMILINGELEPHANT.COM

4. **HUGH BABY'S,** 718 THOMPSON LN., NASHVILLE, (615) 610-3395, HTTPS://WWW.HUGHBABYS.COM

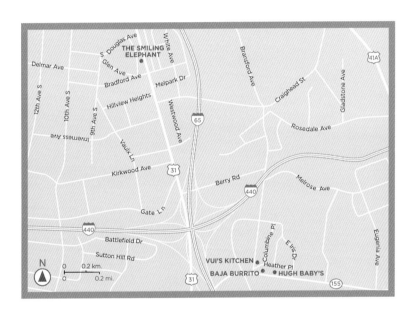

Berry Hill and 8th Avenue

Low-Key Eats

While this neighborhood isn't quite as glitzy as other spots in Nashville, it has plenty of gems scattered throughout. While not a tourist destination per se, its convenience to downtown and other neighborhoods make it a popular place to live and work. It is home to many artists and musicians and is known to have the most recording studios in Nashville. If you find yourself driving around, you'll find this to be true! Alongside the musical influence, you'll find a very diverse food scene, with authentic cuisines all around you. My favorite places to eat here include one very traditional Thai restaurant, a fast-casual Vietnamese, a real good burger joint, and one that serves California-style Mexican.

1

VUI'S KITCHEN

Y'all, never say no to Vietnamese food. Pho, rice bowls, bánh mì, Vietnamese iced coffee? Yes, please! The very fresh and bright **VUI'S KITCHEN** first opened in the Berry Hill neighborhood in 2012 and surely spiced things up in Nashville. The fast-casual restaurant is both authentic and approachable. Their menu items feature whole foods, lots of herbs, and no MSG. With its welcoming nature and patron-friendly menu, Vui's has made the city fall in love with this cuisine.

My go-to order is very hard to break. I am a big fan of the rice bowl with jasmine brown rice, finely chopped lettuce, arugula, thinly sliced carrots and cucumber, fresh herbs, chile lime dressing, and topped with a choice of meat; I wholeheartedly recommend the lemongrass pork belly. If you're looking for that warm fuzzy feeling on a chilly day, you're in need of the original pho. Twelve-hour bone broth with tender beef slices, rice noodles, bean sprouts, onions, fresh herbs, jalapeño, and lime is just the thing to get you where you need to be! The broth really speaks for itself here, and the fresh and crisp toppings give just the right amount of flavor without too much distraction. If you've never had a Vietnamese iced coffee, your time is now. Chicory and French roast with sweetened condensed milk, served cold brewed or slow dripped over ice should be the sweet and caffeinated ending to your time at Vui's.

2 BAJA BURRITO

This welcoming Southern California Mexican joint exists to bring the people a real taste of the Baja lifestyle. This fast casual build-your-own style of Mexican is a favorite among us Nash-villians. Sometimes, you just don't have to fluff up the things that already taste good. This locally owned, independent burrito shop is here for your fulfilling lunch fix and cheerful, stress-free dinner outing with friends and family, and offers indoor and outdoor seating.

BAJA BURRITO has the essentials: tacos, burritos, and taco salads. Choose your rice, beans, and options of chicken or fresh veggies. For you burrito folk, you even have quite the assortment of chipotle, spinach, or classic flour and corn tortillas to wrap up your bundle of love. I can't resist the opportunity for a really good salad with all the toppings. Their Blackened Salmon is the house special and just the California energy I need to finish out my day. Grab some pineapple salsa at the self-serve bar and take one of the many bottles of hot sauce off the wall to have the spiciest of times.

3

THE SMILING ELEPHANT

A real, smiley, Thai experience! Seriously, I just ate here and one of the owners could not stop smiling every time he brought us a dish. The laid-back, cozy, quirky quarters are known for affordable, traditional Thai food. The inside of the SMILING ELEPHANT is scattered with photos of family as well as a celebrity guest or two. There are Thai delicacies for sale and lots of plants. The walk-in-only restaurant moves quickly, which makes it a perfect lunch spot for a healthy-ish meal and tea.

As soon as you walk in, you'll likely notice a few tables with iced orange drinks. These would be the Thai Tea, made with sweet milk and spices such as turmeric and cardamom (they don't disclose the full recipe!). Whatever is in it, it is wildly delicious. Moving on to appetizers, it's hard not to start with a bao or dumplings! The ginger dipping sauce is simply amazing, all things spicy and sweet and totally drinkable. As a romaine fan girl, I love getting the Larb Lettuce Wraps (minced pork tossed with fresh cilantro, scallions, onions, fresh squeezed lime, and white rice). Grab a noodle dish or a daily curry special, and you'll be as happy as the people in the land of smiles.

4 HUGH BABY'S

HUGH BABY'S is a fast casual burger joint brought to you by Pat Martin of Martin's BBQ. His West Memphis roots and commitment to scratch-made, good ole southern cooking has given the people of Nashville the fast-casual burger joint we've so desperately needed. Milkshakes included. The menu and space bring you back to the days of getting a quick and quality burger and fries back in the fifties.

I love this burger. It's not too big, not too small; it isn't messy and it won't make you sleepy if you have it for lunch. It's crispy, saucy, and easy to eat on the go. Outside of the burger I'm currently craving, Hugh Baby's slings gas station–style hot dogs, including ones with coleslaw, chili sauce, and the Pickwick Dog (with grilled onions, jalapenos, mustard, mayo, and their very own BBQ sauce). On Fridays, they serve the famous Slugburger, which was made popular in depression times in northern Mississippi and was typically made with some kind of ground beef or pork, flour, and grits. It can't get more real than that.

Andrew Thomas Lee

Andrew Thomas Lee

Andrew Thomas Lee

THE WEDGEWOOD HOUSTON CRAWL

1. **BASTION,** 434 HOUSTON ST., NASHVILLE, (615) 490-8434, HTTPS://WWW.BASTIONNASHVILLE.COM

2. **DOZEN BAKERY,** 516 HAGAN ST., #103, NASHVILLE, (615) 712-8150, HTTPS://WWW.DOZEN-NASHVILLE.COM

3. **DICEY'S PIZZA & TAVERN,** 425 CHESTNUT ST., NASHVILLE, (615) 964-7022, HTTPS://WWW.DICEYSTAVERN.COM

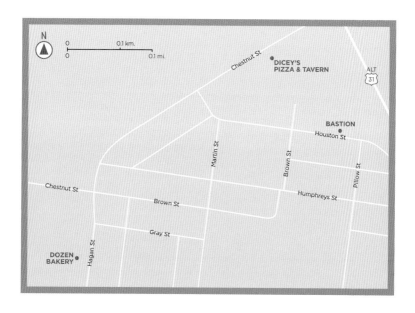

Wedgewood Houston

Cool Bars, Stellar Bakeries

This was a neighborhood I visited first in 2016 and thought Whoa, this is cool! The most popular strip within this neighborhood is called Houston Station, formerly a home to flourishing factories such as Bagwell Preserving Co. and their tasty jams; a tobacco distributor; and May Hosiery, known for sponsoring numerous Jewish refugees during World War II. They worked at the mill primarily making women's socks and stockings. Today, alongside the train tracks and history, you'll find a number of trendy bars, our new soccer stadium not far down the road, bakeries and coffee shops, and contemporary art galleries. The repurposed and mixed-use feel of this neighborhood really shows Nashville's personality.

1 BASTION

If you ever think you're not in the mood for nachos, you're wrong. It's the only item on the menu, and once you have them, you'll understand why. Not only are you enjoying them inside a whitewashed converted warehouse bar, decorated with thrifted furniture and artwork, but you're most likely sipping on a craft cocktail as well. What makes these nachos so good? I'm not exactly sure, but they taste so fresh. Quality chips, queso fresco, black olives, pickled red onion, pickled jalapenos, lime, and a dollop of sour cream, offered with smoked pork or vegetarian chorizo, or how I like it, as is.

BASTION is one of those places that is simply cool, without being pretentious. A place you can hole up in the rain or wander in through their garage door on a sunny afternoon. While I most frequent the big bar, they have a separate very small (and very hard to get reservations for) twenty-four-seat restaurant, complete with its own tiny bar for guests, a pre-fixed menu, and full five-star experience. Until I can get that reservation, meet me at the big bar for nachos and tequila!

2 DOZEN BAKERY

This Nashville bakery nestled between an art gallery, distillery, and a very trendy neighborhood is **DOZEN BAKERY**. The bakery started as a holiday cookie pop-up business in 2009 and did not intend to be much more, but it quickly captured the hearts of the people. They stand by sourcing locally and sustainably, the value of working with your hands, and the quality of ingredients that they use. The line can get a little long, but luckily they have some extra cute bread-themed retail items and merch to shop while you wait, along with an open window to watch their bakers do their magic.

If you love bread, Dozen is a must. I'm talking baguettes, vollkornbrot, French country sourdough, sweet potato sourdough, umami sourdough, challah, sandwich breads, and more unlikely (and incredible) flavor friendships. On top of that, they have an assortment of croissants, pies, muffins, and cookies on the regular. Outside of their bakery, they have a thriving brunch and lunch menu with sandwiches, waffles, salads, and soups. I recently went for the quiche and salad combo, and the way this quiche ruined all other quiches for me is very real. The eggs were so soft and fluffy, completed with an extra smooth goat cheese, herbs, spring peas, asparagus, and the most perfect flakey, buttery crust. Complete your experience with a cortado and a chocolate croissant.

3 DICEY'S PIZZA & TAVERN

This family-friendly pizza joint is for friends and family of all ages. There's plenty of space indoors, on the outdoor patio, and in the yard with the back-bar to serve up fun frozen drinks, natural wine, thin square-sliced pizzas, salads, and appetizers. **DICEY'S PIZZA & TAVERN** has become a home for Nashville soccer fans to watch games and pre-games with shareable pizzas. It's also a great spot for the post–rec soccer game for the kids and parents.

The one appetizer you can't miss here is the Fried Pickles and Peppers. I don't know how, but they managed to create the lightest, crispiest batter, accompanied with homemade dill ranch dressing. Slide through the menu to the salads, subs at lunchtime, and make your way to their pizza. You'll have the opportunity to build your own with a classic tomato, vodka sauce, or parmesan cream (yum). They have all your classic meat and veggie toppings, and the option for vegan cheese and gluten-free crusts. My personal favorite is the Peppy Boy (Old World pepperoni, hot honey, mozzarella, parmesan, wild oregano, tomato sauce, and Calabrian chili oil to give it some shine and spice).

HILLSBORO VILLAGE CRAWL

1. **GREENERY CO.,** 1705 21ST AVE. S., NASHVILLE, (615) 915-1235, HTTPS://WWW.GREENERYCO.COM

2. **PROPER BAGEL,** 2011 BELMONT BLVD., NASHVILLE, (615) 928-7276, HTTPS://WWW.PROPERBAGEL.COM

3. **INTERNATIONAL MARKET,** 2013 BELMONT BLVD., NASHVILLE, (615) 297-4453, HTTPS://WWW.IM2NASHVILLE.COM

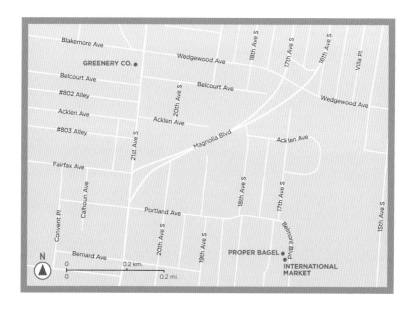

Hillsboro Village

A Cute Little College District

Tucked between Belmont and Vanderbilt University is Hillsboro Village. While in the middle of a college sandwich, it doesn't necessarily feel that way. The main street provides lots of coffee, boutiques, and friendly lunch options for many working people and locals nearby. Over on Belmont Boulevard, you'll notice more college students, but the area is really just very cute. You'll find lots of classic Nashville bungalows, small businesses, and friendly faces. The location is pretty unbeatable when it comes to being in the center of Nashville. Within minutes, you can visit 12 South, Music Row, Edgehill Village, and more. While there's plenty to explore in this area, my top recommendations here are picks that I visit over and over again. So if you're in the mood for really good Thai, a New York bagel, and Nashville's premiere salad and grain bowl, you should definitely visit!

1

GREENERY CO.

Salads! Grain bowls! Health! For much too long, Nashville has been deprived of fast-casual healthy food. Someone actually described Nashville as a "salad desert" to me once, and that really stuck. Sister duo Courtney and Whitney both spent their undergrad days at Vanderbilt and felt the pains of not having any healthy and convenient dining options nearby. After a few months in other cities with a salad chain on every corner, the idea sprouted. They graced the neighborhood of Hillsboro Village with the ever-so-picturesque **GREENERY CO.** The exterior has the sweetest European, cottage feel, and the interior is freshly designed with high ceilings, natural woods, and the most perfect pops of light green. Behind the ordering counter, you'll see their daily deliveries artfully displayed in wicker baskets.

Take your pick between a pre-made salad, warm grain bowl, and seasonal soups! As you can expect, Greenery Co. thrives at lunch time and has some very loyal customers. One of their most popular bowls is the warm Chipotle Shrimp (blackened shrimp, wild rice, avocado, green apple, purple cabbage, cilantro, and crispy tortilla chips with honey chipotle vinaigrette). For the salad side, the Chicken Pesto (roasted chicken, spring

mix, parmesan cheese, cherry tomatoes, roasted broccoli, crispy chick-peas, and fresh basil with pesto vinaigrette) is a great way to go. Oh, and by the way, they have the best chocolate chip cookies. Always add the cookie . . . always!

PROPER BAGEL

My Northeastern transplant soul lives for **PROPER BAGEL**. The family-owned eatery has forty years under its belt of traditional baking. Bagels are (obviously) made from scratch, kettle-boiled, and baked in a stone-lined oven. True, classic perfection. The space is quick, quaint, and ready to roll as soon as you walk in. So grab a Dr. Brown's Cream Soda, a black and white cookie, and drool over the lineup of cream cheese you're about to encounter.

I tend to lean toward a nice, salty breakfast after a night out. I love a good bialy (a less fluffy cousin of the bagel) or a salt bagel. Plus lox cream cheese with capers, add onion, maybe tomato. It's a build-your-own-bagel experience, which I very much appreciate. You can always get a little crazy with jalapeno bacon or dill pickle cream cheese. Don't worry, sweet tooths, strawberry shortcake and classic blueberry cream cheese is also ready for you. And, maybe I'm focusing too much on cream cheese here (can you blame me?), but their open-faced toasts, egg sandwiches with the most incredible tomato jam, matzah ball soup, and all of the sides and pastries are also at your fingertips.

3 INTERNATIONAL MARKET

The original **INTERNATIONAL MARKET** had been serving the people of Nashville on Belmont Boulevard since 1975, run by Patti and Win Myint. Pioneers of their time, the couple introduced Thai food to Nashville, and provided a comfort spot for generations of students, neighbors, and the whole city. I will miss being told how to properly enjoy the meal they'd place in front of you, especially when you didn't ask. The type of place where you'd go to the cash register

to order and let her know you had a cold, and she'd fix something up for ya. Two years after selling the original location to the university she loved so much, Patti passed away. Daughter Anna (the front-of-house queen) and son Arnold (chef and judge on Food Network's *Chopped*) reopened International Market across the street from its original location. There's so much love in this story. Staff who were there in 1975 are still there! But let's get to the food!

Arnold has given some serious glam to the brand-new International Market without sacrificing the tradition. You can still order from the hot line for a quick and easy lunch with all the sides, or order off the menu at the register. The space is super colorful, with booths and tables spread throughout. The Shu Mai is an absolute need to order, perfect little dumplings to get you excited for what's to come. I can't guarantee this menu will stay the same, but I guarantee everything will be magical. Expect to find coconut-based soups with crispy wontons and herbaceous lemongrass, a special take on fried chicken, all of the noodles, and perhaps some jumbo prawns. Stay up to date on the menu via their Instagram.

THE MIDTOWN (MUSIC ROW) CRAWL

1. **HATTIE B'S,** 112 19TH AVE. S., NASHVILLE, (615) 802-5700, HTTPS://WWW.HATTIEB.COM

2. **HENLEY,** 2023 BROADWAY, NASHVILLE, (615) 340-6378, HTTPS://WWW.HENLEYNASHVILLE.COM

3. **WHITE LIMOZEEN,** 101 20TH AVE. N., NASHVILLE, (615) 551-2700, HTTPS://WWW.GRADUATEHOTELS.COM/NASHVILLE/RESTAURANT/ WHITE-LIMOZEEN

4. **PASTARIA,** 8 CITY BLVD., NASHVILLE, (615) 915-1866, HTTPS://WWW.EATPASTARIA.COM

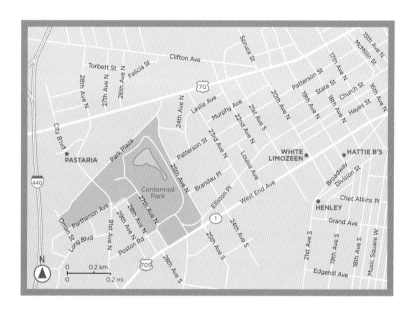

Midtown (Music Row)

Lively Dining in the Heart of the City

While most people head to Midtown to visit a well-known dive bar or two with live music, I'm going to redirect you to where to eat before you decide to stay up too late. This neighborhood is really an extension of Music Row, the street filled with the buildings where all the business gets done. The main attraction of this area is indeed, the bars. You'll find a mix of college students, tourists, and folks who just like to party and sing karaoke. While back in the day, or even ten years ago, this area was once seen as a less obvious choice to go see live music in a more tame setting than Broadway, it has grown up and outward, expanding in retail, hotel, and restaurant options.

1

HATTIE B'S

Two words: Hot chicken. It's one of many things Nashville does best, and **HATTIE B'S** is quite famous for it. This father-son duo started spicing up the lives of Nashvillians in 2012 with their fast-casual approach. Whether you like your chicken southern style (no heat) or "Shut the Cluck Up!!!" hot, you'll be able to

choose what part of the bird you want, put it on a sandwich or leave it be, and pick from classic southern sides such as baked beans, cole slaw, black-eyed peas, crinkle-cut fries, southern greens, or my personal choices, the red skin potato salad and pimento mac and cheese.

Choosing your level of heat is essential to your experience, so play this smart. Nashville's hot level is about ten times hotter than any other city. So, when it says mild, it's actually still quite hot! Calm down the tasty spice with your side of white bread and house-made pickles and a sweet tea. If you make it in for Sunday brunch, lucky you! Get yourself the hot chicken and waffles with a side of cheese grits and a banana pudding for dessert.

2 HENLEY

HENLEY describes itself as a restaurant with "Southern soul and French technique." For dinner service, you'll notice rather quickly that the people are dressed and ready to dine. At the lounge and bar area, you'll meet eyes with a woman above the liquor shelves. The two-eyed mural is a rather edgy touch of art that serves as the perfect backdrop to any cocktail they're whipping up. Other interior moments include black-and-white checkered floors, a wall of antique hand mirrors, and tufted leather seats.

Places like Henley make me really love the South and its history with food. No bean, rice, or cut of pork will ever be treated the same. The kitchen is always switching up the menu to stay seasonal, but you'll always find Southern touches throughout the menu, dishes like an oyster stew with smoked marrow, celery leaves, and cornmeal tuile (a very thin cornmeal cookie). And always an order for me, beef tartare! The one photographed features perfectly toasted white bread triangles, a mountain of pecorino, and cured egg yolk shavings. If beef isn't your thing, you can choose from a perfectly cooked whole roasted chicken, duck and dumplings, or perfectly seared pork shoulders. There is no shortage of fresh pasta dishes or seafood either. And, a fun fact: Henley has a somewhat secret restaurant inside called the Rabbit Hole, where you and one other person can pay a pre-fixed price to dine inside the kitchen for an experiential meal. As they describe it, "a once-in-a-lifetime experience awaits those mad enough to fall down the Rabbit Hole."

Digital Love

3 WHITE LIMOZEEN

Would it really be Nashville without a hot pink Dolly Parton–themed rooftop bar? No, no, it would not! On the top floor of the Nashville's Graduate Hotel, walk through the pearly gates to Dolly Parton heaven. The details of **WHITE LIMOZEEN** are cozy, elegant, playful, and pink. On the outside you'll find white-fringed umbrellas, the governor's pool, 1950s floral print oversized loungers, and one massive sculpture of Dolly's head made from chicken wire. Inside is decked in velvet couches, dramatic chandeliers, sparkles, and grit—basically what you think Dolly's living room would look like.

Naturally the cocktails are all inspired by the famous words of Ms. Dolly. Grab yourself a Queen of the Rodeo (as they describe it, "a gussied-up cosmo") and if you're with a big group, there are massive, model-worthy punch bowls at your service. Food-wise they have a large list from yummy bar bites and light small plates to full, filling entrees. I always appreciate a raw bar. Find a selection of oysters with a spicy mignonette, poached shrimp, the delicacy that is caviar, biscuits, and deviled eggs.

I don't know about you, but when I imagine myself being classy by a pool, there's a shrimp cocktail and champagne next to me—possibly alongside some fancy cheese and gelato. Live your best life!

MJ Geeney

MJ Geeney

MJ Geeney

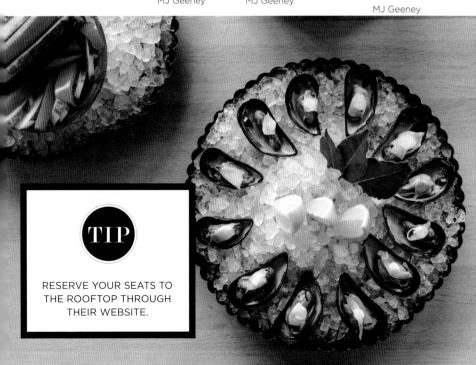

TIP

RESERVE YOUR SEATS TO
THE ROOFTOP THROUGH
THEIR WEBSITE.

4 PASTARIA

"Nashville (sorta close to Italy)" is what they say. They're sorta not wrong! **PASTARIA** opened in Nashville right around the time I was really missing some quality Italian food. I visited rather quickly after taking a gander at the menu, and it did not disappoint! The space is newer and they did a fantastic job creating the warm, modern, neighborhood atmosphere that makes Pastaria a truly wonderful and lively gathering place for friends, dates, and parents!

The best feeling in the world is looking at a menu before getting to the restaurant and knowing exactly what you're going to get. That's how I felt about Pastaria's Pistachio Ravioli. Freshly made ravioli with pistachios (of course), mint, lemon brown butter, and a parmesan-esque cheese. Nutty, creamy, acidic, and bright—a 12/10 dish. On top of their scratch-made pasta list, they have authentic pizza galore, crispy risotto balls, wine on wine on wine, salads, and dessert. I've never turned down a tiramisu, and neither should you.

Pastaria   Pastaria

Pastaria

THE NATIONS CRAWL

1. **BRIGHTSIDE BAKESHOP,** 4907 INDIANA AVE., NASHVILLE, (615) 678-5058, HTTPS://WWW.BRIGHTSIDEBAKESHOP.COM

2. **DADDY'S DOGS,** 5205 CENTENNIAL BLVD., NASHVILLE, (615) 802-8481, HTTPS://WWW.DADDYSDOGS.COM

3. **THE CAFE AT THISTLE FARMS,** 5122 CHARLOTTE AVE., NASHVILLE, (615) 953-6440, HTTPS://WWW.THECAFEATTHISTLEFARMS.ORG

4. **BARE BONES BUTCHER,** 906 51ST AVE. N., NASHVILLE, (615) 730-9808, HTTPS://BAREBONESBUTCHER.COM

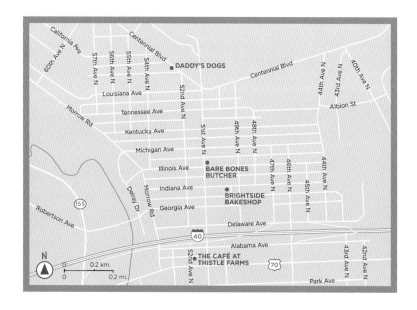

The Nations

Cute Cafes and Hot Dogs

This area in West Nashville has seen a ton of development over the years. It's filled with repurposed warehouses, bike lanes, very intentional housing that feels very community driven, while still holding on to its sort-of animated, funky charm from old buildings. This area is super popular for young professionals for good reason. With lots of green space, walkability, and mixed-use buildings, its own Saturday farmer's market, and plenty of coffee shops, it's a great place to work and play. Here you'll find Nashville's famous hot dogs, an unreal bakery, and a cafe that's doing good for the community.

1 BRIGHTSIDE BAKESHOP

Their motto, Baking Days Brighter, certainly holds true! This sweet little bakery opened in the Nations in early 2020. **BRIGHTSIDE** first began selling their goods at a Saturday morning Richland Park Farmers Market, with a lot of early mornings (I'm talking 2:00 a.m. early) and love for pastries. The hustle was real for owner Andrea Borchers who took her love for a perfect croissant and turned it into her full-time business with a lot of butter and dedication.

You may be wondering what makes these pastries so special, and the answer is just about everything. The perfect crisp, the right amount of butteryness, sweet and savory flavors. I could eat their Churro Croissant every day for breakfast, and then a Three Cheese Brioche for dinner. They also have their croissants in roll form—what?! Get at least a half dozen of these while you're there because they sell out quickly!

TIP

FOR THOSE VISITING WITH A BIG GROUP, I WOULD TOTALLY
RECOMMEND ORDERING SOME OF THESE PASTRIES AHEAD
OF TIME! YOU'LL BE HAPPY YOU DID.

2 DADDY'S DOGS

You may have seen signs around town reading, "Size matters" or "It's okay to be a daddy's girl." And, while you may be slightly taken aback, that's why we love it. This mildly vulgar and late-night take on hot dogs has the after-midnight crowd going wild. If you're leaving the bar, you're looking for a Daddy's Dog. Founder Sean Porter (aka Big Daddy, aka the guy with the most incredible beard) has a pretty neat background of touring with musicians, but his charismatic personality and love for food is what led him to the hot dog industry.

DADDY'S DOGS started serving their dogs in 2015 the old-fashioned way—from a hot dog cart! They began with their carts outside the most popular going-out neighborhoods like Demunbreon Street, Midtown, and downtown. Wherever the people wander. A mix of cheeky marketing and late-night feasters made Daddy's Dogs the relish on top of a perfect evening. They have opened a few brick-and-mortar stores over the past few years,

including inside both the Titan's and Nashville Soccer Club's stadiums. Their flagship location is in the Nations. You'll find Daddy's Dogs located at a glowed-up old gas station, serving dogs through the window and folks eating and drinking forty-ounce Miller High Lifes under the carport.

What hot dog should you get? So glad you asked! I often find myself trying the classic first so I can taste all the real and good flavors of the bun and dog. So if you're into that too, by all means, go for the Lone Wolf (hot dog, mustard, ketchup, and relish). That being said, cream cheese on a hot dog blew my mind. The Seattle with its cream cheese, grilled onions, and

sriracha is a melty spicy dog you want to finalize your evening (or Saturday lunch). They even recently created a special pizza dog with Nashville's own Doug the Pug at their annual puppy play day festival in Richland Park. Daddy knows no limits, and it serves the people right.

3 THE CAFÉ AT THISTLE FARMS

In 1997 owner Becca Stevens opened her first sanctuary that housed five women survivors of childhood abuse, just like her. The women had made incredible strides, but Becca still saw the struggle to remain financially stable due to employment barriers. It was in 2001 when they began making candles in a church basement, and Thistle Farms was born. Now a pillar in the Nashville community, this amazing non-profit employs and provides housing for women survivors of human trafficking and addiction. They believe love has the power to heal, and trust me, once you step inside the CAFÉ AT THISTLE FARMS, you will feel every bit of love!

The cafe is a beautiful place to meet, sip, eat, and work. When you walk in, you'll notice an absolutely stunning teacup chandelier on the ceiling. The cups represent survivors around the world, and each one was collected or gifted until they had hundreds. You're then on your way to order at the counter from a selection of fresh salads, grain bowls, pastries, quiche, soup, and other light comfort foods. There's no shortage of lattes, tea, or the perfectly purple lavender lemonade. You can also book an official tea service, complete with a tower of sweet and savory pastries by the chef. Stay a while and shop the candles that started it all, homemade lotions and soaps, jewelry, leather goods, and more at the Shop at Thistle Farms, located next to the cafe. Every purchase makes a difference!

4 BARE BONES BUTCHER

Way more than a butcher shop, **BARE BONES BUTCHER** has a top-tier sandwich lineup that can't be rivaled! When you only use house-cured meats, local ingredients from farmers and bakers, and scratch sauces and dressings, you're going to create a truly amazing, seasonal, meaty sandwich.

It shouldn't be a surprise that one of the most talked-about burgers in Nashville is at a butcher shop. I asked them their secret and the answer was simply, "the quality of the meat"! Be sure to get a side of the beef chili, beef fat fries, and collard greens with ham hock to get the full experience. You can also find sandwiches on their everyday menu like Jonas's Famous Bologna with pimento cheese and green relish, their signature po' boy, and an outstanding meatball sub. On Friday and Saturday, they'll have two weekend specials that will always be worth checking out. If you're so inspired by your sandwich, be sure to take a look at the butcher counter and rotating pre-made specials such as queso, pig head pozole, rigatoni bakes, and whatever soups they feel like cranking out that week.

THE SYLVAN PARK CRAWL

1. **BOBBIE'S DAIRY DIP,** 5301 CHARLOTTE AVE., NASHVILLE, (615) 864-5576, HTTPS://WWW.FACEBOOK.COM/BOBBIESDAIRYDIPCHARLOTTEAVE

2. **HATHORNE,** 4708 CHARLOTTE AVE., NASHVILLE, (629) 888-4917, HTTPS://WWW.HATHORNENASHVILLE.COM

3. **ANSWER.,** 132 46TH AVE. N., NASHVILLE, (615) 942-0866, HTTPS://WWW.ANSWERRESTAURANT.COM

4. **LOLA,** 4401 MURPHY RD., NASHVILLE, (615) 830-5499, HTTPS://WWW.LOLANASHVILLE.COM

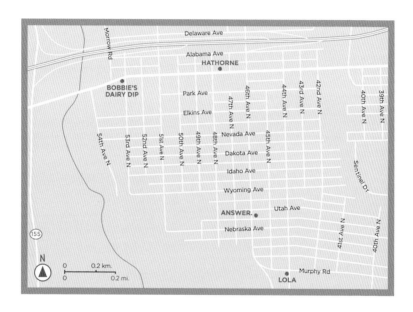

Sylvan Park

Neighborhood Charm and Elevated Happy Hours

This quiet, dreamy little neighborhood does not slack in the food department. This family-friendly area is filled with distinctive historic charm, the popular McCabe Park and golf course, and very walkable streets. While quieter than other parts of the city, it is an extremely desirable place to live and have a really good meal. Mark these next few spots when you're looking for an elevated happy hour and appetizers or a special night out with a loved one.

1

BOBBIE'S DAIRY DIP

If you like retro drive-ups and soft-serve ice cream, you're going to want to go to **BOBBIE'S DAIRY DIP**. Driving down the main road of Sylvan Park, you'll spy an all-outdoor dining area with electric-green and pink picnic tables, and a fifties-looking cartoon on top of this lively building that feels like it's straight out of Grease. Bobbie's has been operating since 1951 at this very location, and there's no doubt that it still holds its charm as Nashville's most endearing pastime.

This old-fashioned dairy bar serves hand-dipped cones in chocolate, peanut butter, cherry, or butterscotch; banana splits; malt shakes; frozen dipped bananas; and my personal favorite, a classic soft-serve vanilla with rainbow sprinkles. Stop by for just ice cream or make it a meal! Their classic angus patty cheeseburgers, hot dogs, and hand-cut fries are pure perfection on a warm Nashville evening. You can even find sweet potato fries, veggie burgers, a variety of specialty chicken sandwiches, and burgers at Bobbie's as well.

2

HATHORNE

Step inside **HATHORNE** and leave your worries at the door. Formerly a fellowship hall, this space retains many elements of the historic church, such as the 1889 communion rail reimagined into a divider between tables, and the church pews for seating. The rich colored wood, white brick walls, and navy and gold accents bring a special warmth to the dining room. Chef John Stephenson created a colorful menu inspired by his travels and experiences with cuisine from all over the world. Enjoy this vegetable-forward, shareable menu with your closest friends and family. Perfect for a happy hour, date, birthday, and anniversary. The menu feels very universal, seasonal, and unique all at once.

In a recent menu, I couldn't pass up the Crispy Goat Cheese, topped with radish, herbs, and honey ferment. There are some amazing shareables, too, such as their Roasted Golden Beets with tahini and charred green onion puree, parmesan, and olive oil. The menu is separated by small plates, and large plates. A distinction I appreciate. Enjoy a fine dining version of a schnitzel, a pasta dish, and a few rotating meatier dishes such as king salmon or Wagyu. So bring ya mother, bring ya father, bring ya co-worker! There's even a nicely sized patio for outdoor seating for an idyllic, quality brunch.

3

ANSWER.

Nestled among the bungalows of picturesque Sylvan Park, **ANSWER.** seamlessly blends in as the neighborhood's designated evening out. Their food matches their atmosphere, which is sophisticated and romantic. Expect classic seasonal dishes reinvented with a little spice.

There's nothing I love more than a good happy hour. Their bar-top specials happen Monday through Saturday with a menu that has everything for $5.00. Wine, shareables, everything. Get one of each! Their dishes are absolutely dreamy, herby, veggie-forward, hyper-seasonal, and filled with combinations you never quite thought of, but will certainly fall in love with, such as the panzanella, which is a fantastic dish of butternut, tomato, kale, pecorino, currants, croutons, pecans, and balsamic vinegar. I am also a big

pasta lover, so if you're into a delicate carb dinner like spaghetti with bay scallops, arugula pesto, walnuts, pecorino, and lemon, get yourself a glass of red and set the mood at answer.

4

LOLA

Minimalist, but cozy. The new tapas bar could not be a better complement to the neighborhood. Perfect for a date night, girls' night, or just wanting to grab a seat at the bar to wind down with some good wine and unfamiliar appetizers in a trendy environment. **LOLA** is your girl!

In this truly impressive space, you'll find things such as warm olives, fried artichokes, the best spicy potatoes on Earth, and larger plates featuring whole fishes, pork shanks, and charred octopus. Everything is sophisticated and truly a journey to Spain itself. Whether you consider yourself an adventurous eater or not, Lola is a no-brainer. You are guaranteed a dinner that's an exciting, relaxed, and delicious experience. Oh, and get the flan—trust me!

Acknowledgments

To my husband Tim, thank you for eating all the leftovers throughout this journey. Without your stomach, detail-oriented tendencies, and belief in me, this book would not have been possible. I love you (way) more than a chilled red and oysters. Cheers to us!

Index

About the Author

Lifelong foodie **HOLLY STEWART** lives, eats, and works in Nashville, producing content and managing social media for a variety of hospitality businesses. The New England native grew up with a natural love of seafood, but once she discovered the southern lifestyle of backyard smoked barbeque, banana pudding, and fresh oyster roasts, she became a southerner for life. She is thrilled to be able to take you on a tour of her home, and in her opinion, unbeatable eating destination: Nashville!